Choose a topic and start to practise writing. Each booklet has a theme to help you start to write…stories, reports, articles, letters and many more. Start collecting them now.

Guinea Pig creative writing booklets also provide extra practice for children who have completed:

- Creative Story Writing ISBN: 9780955831508
- Persuasive Writing & Argument ISBN: 9780955831515
- Information Writing ISBN: 9780955831522

They are for:

* children who are working at Key Stage 2 of the National Curriculum, levels 3-5 (in Years 5 and 6 of primary school),
* children who are working at Key Stage 3, levels 3-5 (Years 7 and 8 of Secondary School).

They provide practice for all 9-13 year olds, especially children taking 11+ examinations.

© **Copyright 2011**

This pack may not under any circumstances be photocopied, without the prior consent of the publisher.

Written by Sally A Jones and Amanda C Jones

Published by GUINEA PIG EDUCATION

2 Cobs Way,
New Haw,
Addlestone,
Surrey,
KT15 3AF.

www.guineapigeducation.co.uk

Let's **learn** to *write* <u>non-fiction.</u>

When you *write non-fiction*, <u>**you may write**</u>:

- information leaflets

- letters

- reports

- instructions

- diaries

<u>**You must decide**</u>:

1. Who will be my target audience?

2. Who will read this writing?

3. What is the purpose of my writing?

The way you write will depend on what form your writing will take. If it is a letter, you will lay it out in a special way.

Decide:

The form - *an information letter from the head teacher*

The audience - *parents*

The purpose - *to inform parents of a change to the school timetable*

It is a formal letter so it needs to be written in the language of a newsreader.

Plan your non-fiction writing:

PARAGRAPH 1 • Introduce your topic. Write down some facts about your chosen subject.	**Remember:** Use: • facts • opinions • opinions in facts.
PARAGRAPH 2, 3, 4... • Write down the points you want to make in order. • Include some evidence.	• Use connectives or conjunctions: - *and or but (to join compound sentences)* - *or, so, if, when, while, after, before, because, unless, until, whereas, although (to join complex sentences)* - *use pronouns - who, which, whose, what, that* - *to link ideas use - firstly, later, therefore, on the other hand, at that moment, by this time, next, soon...* • Use a range of sentences – simple, compound and complex sentences
Conclusion • Draw all your ideas together in a conclusion.	• Make personal comments

A new, trendy head teacher has come to Rushford school. She wants to make some big changes to the school day.

Read the letter she wrote to the parents of Rushford High School.

Rushford School

EAST RUSHFORD ROAD, RUSHFORD, RT12 8BH

T: 020 7651 5033 E: office@rushfordschool.org.uk

Rushford School,
East Rushford Road,
Rushford,
RT12 8BH.
8th September 2015.

Dear Parents,

You may already know that our school is considering making some big changes to the timetable. We have been discussing a more fun approach to learning and we are writing to you today to see what your views are.

In September, the school will open at 10.00am. This is a very late start, but it would mean that the children wouldn't have to get up so early, especially those who use public transport. At this time, there will be no traffic jams because everyone will already be at work.

In the morning, there will be a school assembly, which will last for thirty minutes and will give children the opportunity to do presentations of their schoolwork. Following this, the children will go back to their tutor groups, where they will each have their own computers on which to learn. There will be programmes in every subject, such as maths, literacy and science, so each individual can work through the levels at his or her own pace. The teachers will be there to discuss any problems.

In addition to this, there will be an afternoon session, which will start at 2pm. The teachers will organise practical classes in science and technology, with hands on activitles to help children learn. Every child will learn to play a musical instrument. There will be art and craft opportunities, enabling the children to paint, do pottery or sculptures.

In social studies, the teachers will organise more outings, including fieldwork and visits to historic places and archaeological digs to take place during the term.

We are planning to close the school on Wednesday afternoons, to give pupils the opportunity to participate in local sports clubs – maybe to learn windsurfing or even horse riding.

There will be no daily homework diary to complete. Instead, the teachers will e-mail the pupils project work they can do. You will be able to choose for your child to join the homework (after school) club, where teaching assistants will help them with their work.

You must understand that these plans are still in the early stages, but the school governors are meeting next week to discuss them. Please write and say what you think about the changes or if you prefer the school the way it is.

Yours sincerely,

Miss Day

Miss Day
Headmistress

Pretend you are a mum or dad of a pupil in the school. Write a short e-mail, saying whether you approve or disapprove of the changes.

School Changes

What **do** the *parents* think and why?

Is 10.00am too late to start school? Why?

I think such a late start is shocking. Why do children need so much sleep? They should be going to bed early so they are not tired in the morning and can get up bright and early to start the new school day...

Do you think children should learn on a computer at their own pace?

I'm not sure if the children would concentrate learning on their own. They may get bored and mess around with their friends if they are not supervised properly. They might waste their time on social networking sites.

I think it is laziness on the part of the teachers. They should be teaching the children and not relying on a computer. Young people spend too much time just sat in front of a screen, watching TV or playing computer games at home. They should not be doing the same at school.

Should your child have homework?

"I feel that homework is very important for a child because it teaches discipline. I do not agree that homework should not be given everyday. "

"I think that less homework will be a good thing. Children are too overburdened with work at the moment. They have no time for themselves."

How long do you think assembly should be? What should it contain?

I am glad to see that school assembly has been included in the new school timetable. It is a tradition that has been going on for years. Giving children the opportunity to participate is a good idea. It will get them use to public speaking and give them confidence...

What subjects do you think they should learn?

I'm worried that the new timetable concentrates too much on sport and art and crafts and not enough on important subjects like maths, english and science. These are the subjects that they will need to get good exam results.

Do you think it is a good idea for children to have Wednesday afternoon off?

I think this is a very bad idea because parents have to work. They will not be able to take time off work to pick up and supervise their children. There will be many children just roaming the streets with nothing to do. It is irresponsible for the school to suggest this. It would be better for children to use this free time to do extra curriculum activities or private study in the library.

Would you send your child to the homework club?

I would definitely send my child to the homework club. It is an excellent idea. They will be able to do their homework in a quiet atmosphere with all the resources they need. If they get stuck and need help, they will be able to ask the teaching assistants...

Imagine that you are the new head teacher of a school. What changes would you make to the timetable or the school day? Write a formal letter to the parents explaining the changes.

Plan a radical, new school timetable here. Fill in the gaps below.

	Monday	Tuesday	Wednesday	Thursday	Friday
10:00					
11:30					
12:30					
13:30					
14:30					
15:30					

Writing can contain:

FACTS

The new timetable started on the 4th January.

OPINIONS

It is necessary that everyone learns to play a musical instrument at school.

OPINIONS IN FACTS

The children, who were e-mailed projects for homework, found the task difficult to complete.

Read how to write a formal letter to help you write your letter.

Address of writer

Use punctuation

DATE

Address of school (or business)

Dear Parents (*greeting*),

1. Write a short introduction and explain why you are writing.

2. State your points in separate paragraphs.

You can:

- give a reason or some evidence to back up your point of view.

- write an explanation or some comments to strengthen your argument.

3. Write a conclusion. Summarise the main points of your message again.

- Use 'Yours faithfully' for Dear Sir or Madam. Use 'Yours Sincerely' for Dear Mr or Mrs

Now write a formal letter to the head teacher, saying what you think about the new school timetable. You are writing to argue. Remember to write in paragraphs – each new point in a separate paragraph.

We say, give your **point**, include **evidence** and make **comments** (PEC). Give your point, include evidence and explanation (PEE).

3 Oakhill Drive,
Rushford,
RT45 4DF.
23/09/2020.

Dear Mrs. S. Green,

I am writing to complain about ....

....

....

....

Firstly, I would like to point out that 10am is much too late to start the school day. Schools, that have experimented with a late starting time, have found that children stay up late watching TV and lay in next morning. They get up at the last possible moment. Their parents will be out at work and they won't get any breakfast. Medical experts state that hungry children who have not had sufficient sleep, will not be able to concentrate at school. It would be better if they went to bed by 9pm, so they can arrive at school next morning at 7am and eat breakfast before they start lessons.

....

....

....

....

....

....

....

....

....

....

Write a recount, story or diary entry about the first day at your 'new school' with its different sort of timetable.

Here are some ideas to help you.

1. Introduce yourself and your schoolmates. Build up characters.

    - Describe the setting of the school.

    - What is the new head teacher like?

    - What changes does she intend to make to the timetable?

    - Why?

2. Describe the first day of the new timetable.

    - Describe what you did on the first day.

    - Include some details about the different subjects.

    - Explain what happened: arriving at school, in assembly, classes and

      outings.

    - What problems occurred?

    - Was there a major complication?

    - What happened?

    - Build up tension or suspense?

3. Think what could happen.

    - What was the outcome of the first day?

    - How were the problems resolved?

    - What did the pupils think?

    - What did the teachers think?

    - What did you say to your family?

    - What did you write in your diary?

Use your imagination to think up some interesting details. Try using humour.

The New Timetable

It was the first day of Miss Day's new timetable at my school, Rushford High School. The new head teacher was making some radical changes. She was proposing that school opened later, at 10am and that students worked through computer programmes for their lessons, at their own pace. During the afternoon, she had planned lots of different activities. Everyone cheered when they heard that the school would be closed on Wednesday afternoons, but they were even more delighted when they heard that homework diaries were to be abolished. Miss Day, the new head, was going to be very popular indeed.

On the first morning of the new timetable, I was enjoying a lay in, that is me Jemima Johnson. It was very cosy in bed.
"Don't forget to get up and go to school," shouted mum up the stairs as she dragged my brother and sister to the car. She would drop them off at primary school on her way to work. I replied dozily,
"Ok mum," but then I rolled over and went back to sleep.

"Ah!" What was that? A drill? Some men were digging up the road. I looked at the clock. It was 9.27am. "Oh no! I've overslept," I said to myself, "I have to be in school by 10am." Now I shot into action, threw on my uniform, swallowed down one of those chewy breakfast bars and dashed out of the door. I waited at the bus stop. The bus came surprisingly quickly... but, of course, the traffic had built up heavily, because of the road works. My head was buzzing with excuses that I could give to Mr Carson. I was late for school. How could I avoid a detention on the first day of the new timetable?

"Oh no," I whispered to my friend Gemma. "I've missed the new school assembly and I had some work to show. Miss Rowe asked me to do a presentation of my history project yesterday, and I stayed up late to finish it."
"How late - midnight?"
"Well, I didn't start until I'd watched Westenders, but it was quite late."
"That's probably why you slept in," she giggled.

It was lesson time. I was sitting in front of my computer, looking at the choice of subjects. I could choose my subjects in any order. Which one should I choose first? I felt perplexed. This was more difficult than I imagined. "Well, they've all got to be done sometime," I said to myself, so I chose the algebra programme in maths. I logged on to my computer and... "Oh no! Sir," I called out to the teacher. "I can't get my computer to work. It's crashed." He walked slowly over and stared at the blank screen. Then, he looked at Harvey's screen. "Oh dear," he shouted. "It looks like the whole system's gone down." Then he said, "Class seven get out a reading book or some project work. I've got to pop out and get the technician."

It was the afternoon, of the first day of the new timetable. Unfortunately, there had been a few hitches. A rumour was going round the school that a certain girl had managed to cause a small explosion in the chemistry lab. She had mixed two chemicals together. I'm not too sure which ones, because science is not my best subject, but the block where the labs were had to be evacuated.

The new timetable had not got off to a good start in other subjects either. For a start, there was a din coming from the music room – a banging, a clattering and so many discordant notes, that Miss Ross ran out of her class screaming. "Turn off that racket or I will resign immediately. " In technology, a girl had apparently sawn off the leg of a chair - in art a boy had spilt a full tin of paint all over the floor, while so many brushes had been piled into the sink that the plug hole had blocked and the rising water had caused a flood on the floor.

But how were the children doing who had ventured out on a school trip? There had been a few hiccoughs here too. The rowdy bunch of children in Seven S had got far too over exited at the thought of their field trip in social studies. They had been fighting and throwing things on the coach and had exasperated the coach driver. Then, Amelia had been sick. On arrival at the nature reserve, Jasmine had picked a bunch of rare flowers for her mum, while her long suffering teacher had hauled Joe out of the lake and inspected his ripped uniform. Could things get any worse? At the museum, for history, Tara was tempted to pick up a precious pot from the fifth century BC, somehow she managed to lift it from the glass case. It was only for a moment, so she could say she had held an ancient relic, but it slipped slowly from her grasp and went crashing down onto the floor in several pieces. The museum said the school must pay for it to be restored – but I think that is out of order. The museum should not have put valuable things around children.

At last the bell rang because it was home time. What a relief! I had opted out of homework club so I arrived home with nothing to do except turn on the T.V. There was nothing interesting on, only tiny tots T.V. What should I do? I really missed my homework. I looked for my mobile to ring my friends but it needed charging. My mum burst through the door, having just picked up my brother and sister from the minder.
"How did the new timetable go?" she asked enthusiastically.
"Cool," I muttered glumly.
"You don't sound convinced," replied mum.
"Well if you really want to know"... I paused but then it all started to pour out of my mouth. "I am not sure I like the new timetable. In fact, I don't like it at all and I might even change schools. I miss the old style of teaching. I miss watching Mr Virdee scribbling out math's problems on the white board. I miss Miss Rowe, the history teacher, droning on about William the conqueror. I prefer to write down my work in exercise books. In fact, I quite like it when strict teachers shout, "Sit down!" "Keep the noise down!" I miss all that discipline stuff. Mum looked concerned.... Secretly I was looking forward to Wednesday afternoon. I had chosen horse riding as my special interest. I didn't think I'd be particularly good at it, as I'd heard that standing in the saddle makes your muscles ache. Besides this, I'm scared of heights and horses are quite big. In fact, I'm scared of horses.

Can you answer these questions about the text?

1. Who was Miss Day?

    ....

    ....

2. What changes had she made?

    ....

    ....

    ....

3. What noise startled the writer when she was in bed and what did she realise?

    ....

    ....

    ....

4. What caused the traffic congestion?

    ....

    ....

    ....

5. Why do you think her head was 'buzzing with excuses'?

    ....

    ....

    ....

6. What problems arose in school on the first day of the new timetable?

    ....

    ....

    ....

7. What problems occurred on the school trips?

    ....

    ....

    ....

7. Why were there so many problems do you think?

....

....

....

8. How did the writer feel when she arrived home?

....

....

....

9. What would it be like to organise your own day? For example, choosing which subjects to study and in which order?

....

....

....

....

10. What is your ideal school day?

> *To have your day organised:*
> - *to have teachers teaching subjects*
> - *different rooms and times for subjects and after school activities (normal school day)*
>
> *To have a day that is not structured or organised:*
> - *you study when you feel like it*
> - *there's no order*

....

....

....

....

....

11. Is homework necessary? Write down what you think?

....

....

....

....

An interview with the children of Class 7S about the new school timetable

Pretend that you are in Class 7S. What did you think of the new school timetable?
Write the answers.

- What time did you get up?

- Was there less traffic congestion because you travelled to school later? (No, because the road had been dug up and there was more traffic than usual.)

- Do you think it is good to have a school assembly?

- What time do you think school should start and finish?

- Should you have Wednesday off and go to school on Saturday?

- If you had to plan your own timetable, which subjects would you choose to do and why?

- Which subjects would you leave out?

- Should all learning be done on a computer so nobody has to write anything down any more?

- If you had the choice, which musical instrument would you learn to play?

- If you were a class teacher, which places would you choose for your class to visit?

- Which after school clubs would you provide?

- How would you plan: the morning, the afternoon, a Wednesday afternoon?

- If your head teacher changed the school uniform, what would you like to wear?

What do teachers and pupils think
of the new school timetable? Add
your own comments

What would you do if you had Wednesday afternoon off?

wind surfing	*rowing*	*canoeing*	*dance*	*street dancing*
wake boarding	*horse riding*	*golf*	*running*	

Can you think of any more?

Write a story about having Wednesday afternoon off.

What were the choices available?
What did you choose?
Why?
Who went with you?
Who was the teacher?
What did you do in your first session?
What did you learn?
Did you learn quickly?
What did you achieve?
Did anything go wrong?
How was it resolved?

Tell the story in a few lines.

An irate Dad writes a letter to his MP – Mr Percival Gore. He sets out his point of view in a letter. Read the letter.

42 Garden Close,
Rushford,
RG15 4AE.

Dear Mr Gore,

I am writing to say that I am disgusted by the new timetable at ... which they started at the beginning of the term.

The new head teacher writes that it would be better for children to start school at 10am to ease traffic congestion. Surely, it would be much healthier for all the children to walk to school, because it is essential that they get plenty of exercise. Secondly, why not start school before the rush hour – maybe at 6am. This would be sensible, because all children would be safe in school, when people drive to work. As there would be less traffic on the roads, there would be fewer traffic jams and less incidents at peak times.

The school says that learning should be fun so that children will present their own assemblies and plan their own lessons. I do not agree with this at all. In fact, I have never heard of anything so ridiculous. Children should not be given so much choice. They need to be taught discipline, so when they go out to work, they will be able to follow instructions. Teachers are paid to teach children. In my day, they stood in front of the class writing on the board. Everyone worked at a fast pace or else there was detention, for the whole class. Isn't it still important for children to learn to sit and listen?

Finally, I've heard that the school are going to give the children a chance to learn practical skills, like horse riding and sailing – so they will need to have Wednesday afternoon off. How deplorable! What are weekends for? What's more, if the children are having so many outings at school, there won't be anywhere for their parents to take them in the holidays. In my opinion, learning should not be fun, because I think children need to learn to do reading, writing and maths.

I look forward to hearing your response.

Yours sincerely,

George. D. Buckingham

Write a letter of your own.

You are an angry Dad. Write a formal letter to your MP.

1. **Write an introduction...**

   *I am writing to say that I am...
   (disgusted, infuriated, angry,
   shocked)*

2. **Write the counter argument sentences...**

   The head writes that it would be better for children to start at 10am because...

3. **Argue against...**

   I am not convinced this change will work because...

   The school say that learning should be fun, so children will plan their own work...

   I do not agree with this idea. In fact, I've never heard anything so... (ridiculous, outrageous, preposterous)

   Finally, I've heard that the school are going to give children a chance to learn practical skills like...

   This is deplorable! In my opinion...

Ideas from Mr Angry
(note the ideas are not in order)

- Learning must **not** be fun.

- Teachers must work harder.

- Children need discipline for work later on.

- Children who don't work, should get detention.

- Teachers should concentrate on reading, writing and maths.

- It is not good to have too much choice.

- Practical skills can be learnt on the weekend.

- Parents organise out of school activities.

- Parents take children on outings.

- School should start earlier (6am) before the busy rush hour.

- An early start would avoid traffic jams and incidents.

- It is healthier for children to walk to school.

Now, write some e-mail replies from different parents. Remember: people will see things differently and have their own opinions.

Here are some examples of different people:

- parents who both work long hours away from home,
- a mum who does child minding,
- a parent who has no job.

<table>
<tr>
<td>

Write a reply from a teacher, like Miss Ross.

....

....

....

....

....

....

....

....

....

</td>
<td>

Write a reply from a working parent.

....

....

....

....

....

....

....

....

....

</td>
</tr>
<tr>
<td>

Write a reply from a stay at home parent.

....

....

....

....

....

....

....

....

....

</td>
<td>

Write a reply from a school governor.

....

....

....

....

....

....

....

....

....

</td>
</tr>
</table>

Imagine:

Hi Fli Games presents...

VIRTUAL EXPERIENCE
HEADTEACHER

*Set up your own free school.
Plan out the school. Decide on
the zany timetable.*

Maybe...

- *you could install a soft house playground to trampoline your day away.*

- *you will design a water filled school with canals. Kids must travel round from classroom to classroom by yacht.*

- *your classrooms will have no chairs, desks or tables – only fur rugs and lots of pets to cuddle.*

Now design George Buckingham's (the irate parent's) ideal school.

- No fun
- Concentration very important
- Silence at all times
- Strict teachers
- Hard lessons
- Victorian principles – reading, writing and arithmetic
- Ghastly uniform
- Three hours of homework, each evening
- Detention for all bad behaviour (untidy writing, homework handed in late, talking in class, answering teachers back... add to the list)
- 7am start and 6pm finish

Can you think of some more ideas?

Made in the USA
Monee, IL
07 July 2026

56644835R00015